Slaughtering the Calf:

Fighting Trumpism

2.0

"Those who are against Fascism without being against capitalism, who lament over the barbarism that comes out of barbarism, are like people who wish to eat their veal without slaughtering the calf."

— Bertolt Brecht, *Writing the Truth Five Difficulties*

Ron Jacobs

Fomite
Burlingon, VT
fomitepress.com

Millions of people are disappointed that Donald Trump is back in the White House. Many of those millions are indeed quite angry about this fact. Some of us are—dare I say—just plain pissed off. From these tens of millions there are many responses. Let me do my best to list the primary responses I have heard. Firstly, there is the question how did this happen? Quite often, the next turn in the unfolding conversation is to blame someone. The list of those getting the blame includes Black people (especially Black men) who voted for Trump. Next in line are Latino and Hispanic men who voted for Trump. Next on the list as being blameworthy are young voters—either because they didn't vote at all or because they voted for Trump. Some folks looking for people to blame might even include white women who voted for Trump. From there the list of the potentially blameworthy groups of US voters shrinks rather rapidly.

Some of those lamenting the return of Trump don't seem to find this list of people to blame very convincing. In their search for reasons for Trump 2.0 they look at the Democratic candidate Kamala Harris. Their reasons to blame her for her defeat include the idea that Biden should have remained the candidate to her campaign's lack of substantive policy ideas. Others say it is the Biden administration's disgusting support for Israel's genocidal slaughter in Gaza that alienated voters. Still others will argue it was the mainstream media, which insists that it was Harris' failure to address the price of eggs that cost her the election. This latter claim is also one made by some on the "left" side of the Democratic Party. Personally, I believe there's a bit of truth to each of these possibilities. Yet, I remain convinced that each of these reasons ignore the essential misogynistic and racist nature of the Trump campaign once Harris was appointed as the Democratic candidate. That campaign message is why the majority of white voters (57% of white voters according to NBC) voted for Trump. The fundamental racism of the US nation combined with a more general misogyny that is found around the world convinced the majority of the white citizens who voted to vote for the most racist and misogynist candidate available. When combined with the fact that millions of people who voted in 2020 to toss Trump out stayed home, the return of Trump was assured.

The reader may disagree with my opening paragraphs but still be against Trump. That's okay because the focus of this pamphlet is not why Trump is back in the White House but how those who oppose him and his trumpist backers can and should oppose them. I mention his backers because it is the forces behind Trump—the ones that prop him up with money, massage his ego and run his government—whose powers must be opposed and curtailed, if not eliminated completely. Trump is the figurehead, the mouthpiece of a malevolent marriage of white supremacy, christian nationalism, libertarian capitalism motivated by extreme greed, imperialist war and virulent misogyny. He might not even believe every thing the groups and individuals espousing these views say but he's more than happy to take their money and do what they ask. Politics and power are purely transactional in much of Trump's world.

The forces behind him, whom I will call trumpists from now on, are different. Most if not all are ideologues of one variety or another. Let's look at some of the more obvious case. Stephen Miller, who Trump will have as an advisor, is a racist whose hatred of immigrants is commonly understood. It was Miller who instituted the Muslim ban and other such policies during Trump's first time around. Together with "Border Czar" Tom Homan and the head of the Department of Homeland Security (DHS) Kristi Noem, one can be fairly certain that the trumpist immigration policy will be racist, probably illegal and certainly immoral. One can sense the growing fear in immigrant communities and among those churches, non-profits and individuals that work with those communities.

The men and women Trump hopes to install in government departments that deal with the military, diplomacy and intelligence continue the trend of ideology prevailing. Suffice it to say that the potential Secretaries of State (Marco Rubio) and Defense (William Hegseth) are best known for their hardcore belief in the right of the US to intervene wherever it sees fit. Of course, this is not that different from any previous administration. However, what is different is the seeming willingness of both to use US forces at their disposal instead of local ones. Furthermore, especially in the case of Hegseth, is his expressed desire to use the military to enforce the supremacist ideals he is known to hold.

When it comes to those agencies that are supposed to regulate corporate America, the only thing I can say is that there will be very little regulating going on. Every single nominee is a true believer in unbridled neoliberal capitalism and the belief that profit trumps everything else, including honesty.

What Are We Up Against?

I have tried to describe the ongoing situation with what I've written so far. To say the least, it's not looking good. But, what can we do about it? In the face of a seemingly hopeless future, how can we oppose the oncoming fascism? If the authorities reject the law as anything but a tool to oppress their opponents and enforce the wishes of their paymasters, what options exist for those of us in opposition?

Not long after the 2020 election, Robert Reich, who served as Labor Secretary during Bill Clinton's time in the White House, shared an essay by former Turkish journalist Asli Aydintasbas, a visiting fellow at the Brookings Institution in Washington

D.C., on how to oppose Trump and his regime. In the essay Aydintasbas shares her thoughts on opposing what she calls the autocracy of Turkish ruler Recep Tayyip Erdogan, whose authoritarian (and elected) government has been in power for over ten years. The essay is addressed to Democrats and Trump critics. I would like to take a few words to respond to his essay.

The essay begins with a few simple and obvious suggestions: Don't panic, don't disengage, don't fear infighting amongst the opposition and find a charismatic leader to oppose the appeal of Trump. Then the suggestions turn toward what I can only call defeatist—"Skip the Protests and Identity Politics." To begin with, linking these two things together diminishes the former and misrepresents the latter. In addition, the advice makes no sense. Aydintasbas (and Reich, apparently) explain their opposition to street protests like this: "Street protests and calls to defend democracy may be inspirational, but they repel conservatives and suburban America." The essay continues by stating that any grassroots organizing must include an economic message and "showcase the leadership potential of Democratic" politicians.

Identity politics alone, writes the author, will not be enough.

Where do I begin? Let's take a look at the Brookings Institution, which currently employs Aydintasbas. The Institute has been around for over a century. It bills itself as a nonpartisan and independent think tank. Its politics lean liberal and it is a firm believer in US capitalism. Indeed, its board of trustees is composed primarily of corporate executives, while its leadership group is made up of former government officials who have served in various administrations and at different US universities. Their work tends to focus on maintaining the US Empire abroad and the capitalist system at home. It does believe in the US version of democracy for the United States. When it comes to countries overseas, its record on democracy falters, given its determination to expand US capitalist growth—something that occasionally goes directly against democratic reforms overseas.

Next, let's take a quick look at Robert Reich. As noted before, he served as Labor Secretary under Bill Clinton. He also worked in the Jimmy Carter and Gerald Ford White Houses and on Barack Obama's economic transition team. In case the reader is wondering, the economic transition was not a transition from neoliberal capitalism to democratic socialism. However, it did consider ideas supported by Reich like universal basic income and a change in the tax structure that would have the very wealthy pay higher taxes. Reich supported Bernie Sanders in his presidential campaigns and many of his positions would be considered on the left in the Democratic Party. At the same time, his books all share a common theme—US capitalism must be saved. Furthermore, he is a Democrat through and through.

It is not my intention to call out Mr. Reich in this essay. I mention elements of his resume only to clarify why he might post the essay by Ms. Aydintasbas in his ongoing commentary about Trump and his supporters. Like Bernie Sanders and millions of others who oppose trumpism, they are allies for those of us opposing trumpism but positioned further to the left politically. At the same time, I personally do not share these allies' faith that the US political system can sustain another four years of Trump and his fascists in power. I make this statement without equivocation based on the US experience over the years 2020-2024. As the reader knows, those four years were spent trying to recover from the previous four years; four years of trumpist attempts to intensify exponentially the ongoing reorganization of the US political system along ever more authoritarian lines and make the economic system ever more beneficial to the wealthiest US residents. It's not that the Biden administration halted these trends. It did however—in between its funding of wars and genocide—attempt to redistribute some of that upwardly mobile wealth back into the pockets of those who produce said wealth.

Specifically, what we saw during this period were various attempts to redistribute small amounts of the wealth accumulated by the 1% back into the infrastructure of the nation and the pockets of the working class, working or not. The Democrats were able to push through a massive bill which has been used to rebuild transit systems, highways and other public projects, but failed at passing legislation that would have expanded Medicare, food subsidies and helped working people keep up with corporate price gouging in the marketplace. As any shopper probably knows, the cost of food, transportation and housing skyrocketed from 2020 through today. Donald Trump got elected in part because he promised to fix this. It remains to be seen what exactly he means by this promise.

So, what is to be done? To repeat myself, what can we do about trumpism—the US version of fascism? A fascism that is covered in the US flag, hung on the cross of the right wing evangelical Christian church, and championed by the capitalist whose monetary success is accompanied by a hatred of labor unions and the very workers who made them rich. This evolving fascism didn't just happen when Trump got elected in 2016. In fact, it's been developing for some time. One of the more obvious indications of this truth is the volume of literature opposing the fascism of the 1930s, a time when fascists had their greatest successes worldwide. A time when fascists filled Madison Square Garden for a rally whose spirit the trumpists summoned forth in October 2024 and the fascist Catholic priest Father Coughlin poisoned the radio waves in a manner quite similar to the FoxNews and OneAmerica television commentators do today. Of course, it was also a time when the novelist Sinclair Lewis published his antifascist novel *It Can't Happen Here,* which captured the essence of what a particularly US fascism would like. It is eerily similar to the so-called MAGA movement,; the movement I call trumpism.

At the same time, trumpism is different. The reasons for this are many. One is the nature of the media in today's world. This is true both in terms of how the public accesses that media and, probably more importantly, who owns and controls it. Back in the 1930s, television barely existed. Radio was in what is now called the "golden age of radio." Consequently, newspaper circulation was in a slow decline, although it is estimated 39 million US residents still read the daily paper, even though the numbers of newspapers being published had diminished. This was in a total population of around 123 million people, less than half of the US population today. Newspaper ownership was considerably less consolidated than it is today. A very important difference was the fact that there were no computers and personal telephones. Therefore there was no social media. One cannot help but acknowledge the role this format plays in contemporary media consumption.

Ironically, it is a role that is often harmful to the social fabric.

This discussion of media seems to be an appropriate time to bring up the relationship between capitalism and fascism. Let me begin with a definition of monopoly capitalism—the form of capitalism of which fascism is a potential outcome. Perhaps the most straightforward definition can be paraphrased in this way: monopoly capitalism is the highest and last stage of capitalism, characterized by the replacement of free competition among all capitalists with the domination of monopolies as its fundamental feature. The nature of capital is to grow and grow. In order to do so, the larger companies will compete with smaller companies until the smaller companies either fail or are taken over by larger entities. The only competition ultimately remaining is that between the largest corporations, which in turn are usually owned by banks and financial houses that produce nothing but wealth. This wealth is produced with the money and debt of banks, their investors and customers. Without governmental interference, the banks and financial houses will accumulate wealth until (one assumes) the house of cards collapses.

Neoliberalism, or neoliberal capitalism(a more descriptive name) is the contemporary form of monopoly capitalism. Like capitalism before it, its only raison d'etre is the pursuit of profit. History tells us that this raison d'etre brings imperial war, internal repression, poverty accompanied by obscene wealth, corruption at all levels of government, and a never-ending insecurity among most of the world's population. History also tells us that capital is more than willing to cooperate with, and even become part of, a fascist regime. It happened in Germany under Hitler and it happened in Italy under Mussolini. It is happening in the United States as I write. Corporations who quarreled with and even opposed Trump during his first term and his 2020 presidential campaign are now lining up to donate millions of dollars to his inaugural festivities. Jeff Bezos, the owner of the Washington Post, prevented the editorial board of the paper—a conglomeration of warmongering and pro-corporate individuals —from running their editorial endorsing Trump's opponent Kamala Harris in 2024. He followed that censorship by censoring a cartoon criticizing that action. Mark Zuckerberg, the head of all things Meta©, just donated at least a million dollars to Trump's victory party on January 20, 2025. Then of course, there's Elon Musk who not only paid for the final months of Trump's presidential campaign, but has wormed his way into the policy-making circles of the administration. These three billionaires are just the tip of the iceberg. Other corporate and financial donors who used to donate to both parties in the recognition that they are more alike than different are now lining up with their checks in hand behind the aforementioned criminals of capital in a sickening display of obeisance.

This is more than transactional political gift-giving. It is more than the theft of the democracy so many US citizens believe in and think their military forces are protecting when they invade other nations. It's more than simple grift and it's not being done by a foreign government, despite what those who blame Russian President Putin think. This is a purely US invention. It is the takeover of the US government by a relatively small group of individuals whose intentions are clearly stated on their websites and in their statements to the press.

This obeisance goes beyond the donation of millions to Trump and his campaign. In recent months several companies have removed their previous commitment to encourage what is called diversity, equality and inclusion (DEI) guidelines in their hiring. These guidelines rejected discrimination in employment based on race, ethnicity, gender, sexual preference and age—reasonable guidelines in today's world. Once the Supreme Court rejected affirmative action as part of university and college considerations for new students, white supremacist state governors and legislatures began demanding all DEI guidelines be removed from all government human resource functions and agencies. These calls were encouraged by various racist and misogynist individuals and groups backing Trump.

It seems pretty clear even from this brief summary that barely skims the surface of the current situation in the United States that opposing Trump involves much more than merely opposing the man himself. The phenomenon of trumpism (or MAGA, if you prefer) is much greater than Trump or his expansive ego. He may not understand or believe this, but the money movers and the political organizations behind his political success certainly do. Many of his backers in the Christian nationalist movement have called him their modern day Cyrus, the non-Jewish Persian king who led the Jewish people from Babylonia. Of course, this depiction of Trump blends well with their apocalyptic beliefs that lead these worshipers to support Israel and its bloody oppression of the Palestinians and its war with its neighbors.

As for corporate America and the banks that own it, it is the promise of further (even total) erosion of commercial regulation that they hope for. While such a scenario would likely begin with the continued termination of environmental regulations like those preserving wetlands and preventing the use of certain toxins in manufacturing, the fear that the minimum wage might be modified downward for certain workers or even eliminated altogether is not as far-fetched as it once seemed. With a national legislature dominated by trumpists and the top court in the nation similarly constructed, almost any law protecting the rights of workers, women, LGBT, African-Americans and other non-white residents or the environment that once seemed the permanent law of the land can no longer be considered as such. Indeed, when one considers the spate of decisions by the current Supreme Court regarding reproductive choice, affirmative action, LGBT protections and so on, it seems pretty clear whose interests this court represents.

So What Can We Do?

In returning to the essay by Asli Aydintasbas that Robert Reich published on his blog and Facebook page, let me start by stating I reject her rejection of street protests as a means to challenge trumpism. In fact, I want to state as clearly as I possibly can that street protests are the most important part of any oppositional campaign to the trumpist takeover. As a veteran of decades of protest, mostly in the cities, towns, and countryside of the United States, but also in Germany, I can say with certainty that protests matter. They work. They heighten the stakes involved and they keep the power of change in the hands of those who are most affected—the people protesting and those that support them. Ultimately, it is protests that create the most reaction while also providing a forum for those of us not in government or with muted (at best) representation in government. Genuine popular democracy comes from the streets. Capitalist democracy comes from corporate boardrooms and rich people's bank accounts and investment portfolios. Fascism pretends to be the former, but is, in the final analysis, a version of the latter that removes democracy from the equation.

The essence of Asli Aydintasbas' essay is that the Democrats and their supporters can defeat trumpism by staying within the lines of the US electoral and judicial system. While I would never reject the efforts of those who do this, the reader must forgive me if I don't share the conviction that the system that created the trumpist reality can undo it. When I read the emails from the Democrats and their various front organizations celebrating the appointment of 235 federal judges by Joe Biden, I can't help but wonder what those judges can actually do in the face of a judicial system overpopulated by right-leaning judges and laws that mostly prevent anything but right wing choices. I will of course support the lawsuits challenging the executive orders against immigrants and who knows who else almost certain to come once Trump is in power, but I remain convinced it will be the popular outcry in the streets against those orders that will make the most difference in the effort to get those orders repealed.

When it comes to electoral politics, my first inclination is to ignore them in the belief that they are a waste of energy. Practically speaking, however, I know this is not true. Most US citizens engage politically at and only at the ballot box. Given this, it remains important to run candidates that represent progressive values. That being said, the candidates should respond to the popular protest and not the other way around. Workers on strike should not adapt to the wishes and words of the candidates nor should antiwar protesters and organizers modify their demands to suit a candidate with whom they agree in spirit.

I'll share an anecdote to explain what I mean. In August of 1990, the Iraqi military moved into part of Kuwait over a dispute about money Kuwait owed to Iraq for Iraq's military defense of Kuwait during the war between Iran and Iraq that lasted most of the 1980s. Kuwait had been threatened by the government in Tehran and asked Iraq (which was supported by the US government at the time) to guarantee military protection. Iraq did so in exchange for an agreed amount of money, which it argued Kuwait did not pay in full. At the same time, Iraq accused Kuwait of stealing oil from natural deposits under Iraq's territorial surface. After Iraq invaded Kuwait, the US government decided to attack Iraq and began moving hundreds of thousands of troops and massive amounts of military equipment to the region. Some of us began putting together an anti-intervention coalition in Olympia, Washington where we lived. We held a few events and a couple demonstrations locally while also publicizing other events in Seattle and along the west coast of the United States. Naturally, there were lots of meetings. We set up some general parameters regarding how the meetings would be run, what would be the requirements for groups wanting to join the coalition, and so on.

As it became quite clear that the US was going to attack Iraq no matter how much Saddam Hussein's government negotiated and gave up in those negotiations, more elected politicians began to be asked what their position was regarding the impending military action. A few came out strongly against the action, supporting sanctions instead. This approach was debated inside the coalition, with the majority of the regular meeting attendees supporting no military action and no sanctions. Other politicians came out strongly in support of military action and differed only in the nature of that action—regime change or the retreat of Iraqi forces back inside Iraq's boundaries. Most said very little, waiting to see what happened.

On January 15, 1991 the Olympia Anti-Intervention Coalition held a rally in downtown Olympia. Around three thousand people showed up. Many were high school and college students who had walked out of class to attend. I was coordinating the speakers and working with members of our security team to keep an eye out for pro-war types who had been harassing a few of the organizers mostly by phone but also at work. My friend Curtis was the emcee. As the speakers and musicians came and went onstage without any serious problems I noticed an organizer and an aide for the congresswoman representing the district Olympia was in beckoning me from the front of the crowd. I went over and asked what was up. The congresswoman, said her aide, wished to speak. I said that we had a policy of no elected politicians speaking at our rallies. This was about the war, not about politicians. At the time I was quite unclear what the congresswoman's position on the impending invasion was. Curtis came over. I asked him to invite the next speaker up and let them go over their time limit if need be while we sorted out the deal with the congresswoman. To make a long story short, the congresswoman did speak, but was only allowed three minutes and I was to introduce her. The congresswoman agreed to the terms. In my introduction, I told the crowd that the coalition was opposed to letting elected representatives speaking in order to prevent them from using the movement for political gain, but we had made an exception in this case because she had come to the rally as a participant and had promised only to issue a statement against the use of force to resolve the issues between Washington and Baghdad. She did stick to our hastily made agreement. After her brief statement, there were a couple more speakers and then the crowd marched to the Olympia State Capitol, which we entered and occupied for several hours. A couple dozen protesters stayed over night in the chambers. Unfortunately, George HW Bush ordered the attack the next day, bringing what he grotesquely called shock and awe to the people in Iraq's capital city Baghdad.

So, yeah. Street protests and grassroots organizing for those protests with the goal of defeating fascism should be first line of defense in the struggle to come, not the second, or the third, etc. And certainly not the last.

I am not opposed to the general program presented by Ms. Aydintasbas and Mr. Reich. I am, however, unnerved by its timid politics and approach implicit in its reliance on the existing political system in the United States. It seems almost redundant to remind these commentators or the public that Trump's re-election and the return of trumpism to the White House is a result of this system and what are at best its shortcomings, if not its design. What is needed is a popular rejection of the Trump White House and its fascism; not just one led by Democrats in the courts and the legislature. This struggle needs to be waged in the streets, the schools, the workplace and throughout the United States. It's a struggle against fascism, not a battle between the political parties of the elites.

www.ingramcontent.com/pod-product-compliance
Lightning Source LLC
Chambersburg PA
CBHW032057040426
42335CB00036B/489